AROUND HAUNTED CROYDON

BY
FRANCES D. STEWART

A
JOIN'
PUBLICA'
BY
AMCD PUBLISHERS LTD
&
CROYDON LIBRARIES

First Published in Great Britain 1989
by
AMCD (Publishers) Ltd.
PO Box 102
Purley
Surrey
CR2 3YX
and
Croydon Libraries
Copyright © Frances D. Stewart 1989

First Edition 1989
1000 copies

ISBN 0 9515066 0 9 Around Haunted Croydon.

CONTENTS

CONTENTS

LIST OF ILLUSTRATIONS

Cover Design and illustration by Sarah-Jane Stewart
Text illustrations by Graham Mason

PREFACE

Without a sound I opened the door to the attic, the flight of stairs led upwards into the dark unknown. I gripped the torch tightly and crept forward. What were the mysterious sounds that had distracted us nightly since we had moved into our new home?

The outcome of this story, which I will reveal later, aroused in me a curious interest in the supernatural. Wishing to know more, I embarked on a period of research which resulted in this varied collection of stories.

To look at Croydon today is to see a modern town still developing, yet it has been in existence for many hundreds of years. I had hoped to find headless highwaymen lurking in the London Road and phantom colliers damping down their fires with water from the Norbury Brook, but it wasn't to be. So many of Croydon's original buildings have been demolished that it is hardly surprising to find the centre becoming devoid of ghosts. An office block that scrapes the sky or an exhaust-filled multi-storeyed car park are not fitting habitats for self-respecting spirits. Although a few old faithfuls remain, they are more scattered about in odd corners of the town, whilst others enjoy the "good life" of the rural outskirts.

My thanks go to the many people I have met and to those who have taken the trouble to send me their stories. Without them this book could not have been written.

Frances Stewart
Purley, Surrey.
1989

CHAPTER I – CENTRAL CROYDON

Being by far the oldest building in Croydon and situated as it is away from the bustling shopping centre, the **OLD PALACE** suggests a highly desirable residence for ghosts.

The Old Palace, Croydon
'The sound of weeping in the Chapel...'

Originally the manor house of the Archbishops of Canterbury, it went through a long period of neglect. At one time, part of it was used as a factory for washing and bleaching linen, whilst another part was an orphanage. It was during this time that maids reported seeing a sad-eyed woman wearing Elizabethan dress standing at the top of a staircase. She appeared to be in great distress, crying and wringing her hands in despair. It was suggested that it was one of Elizabeth I's maids-in-waiting who had committed suicide when she had a baby

1

out of wedlock and had returned to find her child. This ties up with another story that a baby has been heard crying in the chapel and extra-sensitive people have commented on the strange air of sadness that permeates the building.

Since 1889 the palace has been a school for very much alive girls. Though necessarily adapted to provide an agreeable environment for education, there is enough of the original structure remaining to maintain an interesting historical atmosphere. There have been a number of exorcisms in the past and the staircase on which the ghost was supposed to appear has been removed, so the building has ceased to be a favourite haunt. Mind you, I have been told that some staff are reluctant to visit in the evening and the caretakers prefer to keep away once daylight has gone.

⁂

In close proximity to the Old Palace stands the **CROYDON PARISH CHURCH**. Traffic speeds past continuously, yet it still maintains an air of tranquility. It is the burial place of six Archbishops, but only one has returned in spirit form. This is Archbishop Sheldon and you may consider he had very good reason for doing so. In 1867 the church was seriously damaged by fire and the tomb of the Archbishop was completely destroyed. This must have caused him great distress, because it was soon after that his ghost was first seen. Formerly known as a very happy man, he now wandered around with his arms folded and his head hung in sorrow. He continued his nightly jaunts, usually at about 5.45 p.m. for nearly one hundred years until his tomb was restored in 1960.

With what must have been a great relief to him and to those who witnessed his perambulations, his activity ceased and he was never seen again.

The Parish Church, Croydon:
'A hundred years of melancholy'

This story is well authenticated, but there have also been reports of a lady ghost who walks the South aisle and leaves by a door which is now bricked up, and of another who was seen by an organist to enter by the vestry door and to disappear through the altar.

⚜

In the centre of Croydon there stands the **WHITGIFT HOSPITAL OF THE HOLY TRINITY**, or the Almhouses to give it a more familiar name. A fine Tudor building, it is still used today to house senior citizens, as it was when founded by Archbishop John Whitgift in the sixteenth century.

3

The Archbishop had his own suite of rooms in the building where he would stay when he visited, presumably for administrative reasons. One day a traveller coming up Crown Hill spotted a man on the roof about to climb down a chimney. He dashed inside to raise the alarm, thus enabling the Archbishop's bodyguard to apprehend the intruder on the stairs. A fight broke out, causing the would-be assassin to fall on his own stiletto and to die a bloody death. Surely such an event would merit some form of ghostly manifestation? Unfortunately for me, no.

There is just one story and that is of a previous inmate whose little grey-clad figure has been seen wandering around the quadrangle. Why she returns to her old home I do not know but with its green lawns and glowing flower beds it is a delightful place to be.

⚛

On the corner of George Street, opposite the Almshouses, there once stood the **"GEORGE INN"**. The "National Westminister" now replaces the building, but just up the street, next to an estate agents, a pillar remains which once supported the arched entrance to the courtyard. In the eighteenth century local gossip said that many visitors to the Inn, who chose to stay overnight, were never seen again. They were believed to be killed by the landlady who then boiled their remains in a cauldron thus earning herself the name of "Old Mother Hotwater".

Without doubt their ghosts must have returned to haunt her, but presumably disappeared when the building was demolished, or did they? Maybe a few spirits linger on to drift through that archway when Croydon sleeps.

∴

Built on the site of the **"KING'S ARMS"** is "Goody's Wine Bar". To enter from Park Street is to descend into an atmosphere of warmth and comfort. Tiffany lamps throw an intimate glow over the luxuriously upholstered furniture and two statuesque blackamoors hold their lamps up to the ceiling, which is draped in exotic fabrics. A ghost seems highly unlikely, but a ghost there is said to be.

One member of staff is said to have seen a girl sitting by the foot of the stairs when the bar was closed. When told she must leave, the girl just vanished. Another member of staff thought she heard sobbing on two consecutive days, then the apparition appeared standing at the food counter with her head on one side as if listening to the conversation of a group of young men waiting to be served, but the customers did not see her. I was told by the manager, who had been in residence for some time, that one night his head barmaid fled screaming from the cellar, saying that the ghost had gone past her, then straight through the wall. Such was her fright that she refused to enter the cellar again.

Other events included a pile of glass ashtrays falling to the floor, bottles flying through the air and plates of food appearing to be pushed from the tables without logical explanation. In one part of the bar it is always intensely cold, candles burn down more rapidly than at any other table and there is often a pungent smell of perfume.

On one evening, smoke was seen coming from the woodwork and the fire brigade was summoned, but no evidence of burning was found. Prior to that, there had been a fire described as the work of a poltergeist by a medium called in to investigate. Yet another fire occurred in April 1987. It was a Monday night and the bar had been unusually busy. Did the poltergeist strike again? One theory is that she was upset by having her usual peaceful evening disturbed.

Whether this was the cause or not, the manager and his wife said they were most careful not to cause offence. Having noticed that many of the destructive events had happened whenever they moved a chair from the area beside the stairs which was considered to be "her" place, they made sure it was in position at all times — just in case.

⚛

Ghost stories from hospitals are surprisingly few but I consider this one very interesting. A nurse on night duty at **CROYDON GENERAL HOSPITAL** was sitting at her desk making her report. It was in the early hours of the morning, well before dawn, the silence was as deep as always at that time. Suddenly she heard the swing doors open and the sound of a trolley being wheeled into the ward and then out again. She heard the clatter of cups and water running in the adjoining kitchen. Thinking one of the young men must be playing a trick on her, she went to investigate, but no-one was there. Mystified by the experience she walked quietly around the beds, all the patients slept peacefully except one whose illness was giving cause for concern. As she bent over him to re-arrange the bed clothes and make him more comfortable, she asked if he would like a cup of tea. He smiled and moved his head slightly, "No thanks dear" he replied, almost inaudibly, "The white nurse has just given me one" The next morning he died.

When relating the experience to other members of staff, she was told that the ghost was identifiable as a nurse who had once been in charge of that ward. Her ghost had often returned, usually when a patient was about to die. It is hardly surprising that the nurses avoided duties on the ward if they could possibly help it.

In the **WANDLE PARK** area a victorian house said to be haunted is one of a terrace built on land that had once been a seventeenth century plague pit.

A mother and her two children moved into the house in 1969. After a busy day putting everything into place, they retired to bed, but not, I am afraid, to sleep. As the lights were extinguished, the noises began. First it was footsteps on the stairs, which was unnerving enough, but soon the rattling of chains frightened the family even more. When wailing and blood curdling screams were added to the general cacophony, the mother gathered the children to her and they dashed to the end of the garden. There they spent the rest of the night, huddled together and very cold yet too scared to go back inside. When dawn broke, they crept back indoors, where everything was so normal that the mother wondered if it had all been a nightmare.

For a time nothing happened, but no sooner had they begun to settle down than the noises began again. As the screams increased in volume, the family could stand it no longer and fled in terror in the middle of the night. When asked about the experience later, the mother said it had been like living in a graveyard, and I suppose that's precisely what it was.

⚠

Very often it is a ghost's activities that give cause for concern rather than their appearance. A gentleman now living in Thornton Heath told me of his mother's strange experience. As a child she lived in a small house quite near the army barracks in **MITCHAM ROAD.** She was sitting in the kitchen with her mother, who was ironing, when suddenly her mother put down the iron and stared towards the door. Following her gaze, the child saw the kitchen door rise slowly from its hinges, hang in mid-air, then sink slowly back to its correct position. Though they were both quite shaken, the mother soon recovered herself and, convinced that her husband must have returned and be playing some sort of practical joke, she went to look for him, but the house was empty. The next day they heard that a relative had died at approximately the same time as the mysterious happening.

There was no logical explanation for what had occurred and they have never experienced anything again, but it has remained vivid in their memories ever since.

⚠

As a child I lived in **THORNTON HEATH,** a quiet respectable suburb where nothing happened, or so we thought. In 1938 we were startled to find the area hot news in the notorious "Sunday Pictorial". A poltergeist had become manifest in a neat terrace house quite near Brigstock Road.

Being too young to read, I was unable to gorge myself on the newspaper story as my Mother did, but was highly delighted when she happened to meet the lady who lived next door to the haunted house. From the depths of my pushchair, I listened with mounting excitement to the tales of flying furniture, smashing crockery, wine glasses and eggs and of a huge brass fender which crashed at the bottom of the stairs, having been propelled, it would seem, by an inhuman force. What amused me most was

9

that the invisible spirit was said to have smashed a jar of vanishing cream!

Objects were said to come from cupboards whilst the doors were still shut and, during an impromptu séance with a local medium, a piece of coal weighing several pounds was said to have lifted itself from the grate and sped across the room just missing the heads of reporters brought in to witness the events, before hitting the wall with such force that it left a huge hole. The reporters were sceptical but could find no logical explanation.

Newspapers continued to report the supernatural happenings for some time, but after some serious investigations, it was proved to be a hoax, albeit a clever one. Walks in that area were never quite the same for me after that.

⁂

During the Second World War, Thornton Heath suffered severely from enemy action, but fortunately the houses destroyed were replaced as quickly as possible. A gentleman told me that a lady colleague of his, who is apparently a "down-to-earth no-nonsense" Scot, moved with her family into a new maisonette built on one of the old bomb sites in the **PRINCESS ROAD** area. One evening, soon after she had moved in, she was astonished to see two little children, a boy and a girl, sitting on the landing at the top of the stairs. She asked her children if they had invited friends in, but they said that they hadn't She thought that she must have been mistaken but the next day, as dusk was falling she saw them sitting there again, big eyes staring from pale, sad, faces. This happened so often that she felt she had to confide in a neighbour, who, having lived in the area previously, recognised them immediately. She said that during an air-raid the children had died when a bomb had fallen on their house which had stood in that exact spot.

⁂

Another victim of the war was a church in **WOODVILLE ROAD**, Thornton Heath, which was severely damaged by a bomb. Originally used by the Primitive Methodists, it stood empty until bought by another denomination. As it was rather too big for their purposes, the members decided to demolish part of it, leaving some land for much needed housing.

Visiting the building to see how best this could be executed, one of the members had just walked out into the courtyard when he heard footsteps behind him. He heard a door close and the footsteps cross the hall. Presuming it to be the newly-appointed caretaker he called out his name, but there was no reply. Thinking it must be a stranger, he went back inside but nobody was there. Everything was still in its place, the old, dusty furniture stacked to one side; the old organ, soon to transfer to the chapel at Mayday Hospital, towering over all. Nothing had been touched.

Could that mysterious visitor have been the ghost of an organist, just popped in to play the organ for one last time?

⁂

A public house very much of the present but having strong links with the past is the **"WHEATSHEAF INN"** at

11

Thornton Heath. It was built in the eighteenth century as a coaching inn where passengers could take refreshment whilst their horses were watered in the pond. I found two versions of what could be the same story, so for reasons of interest I will relate them both.

The Wheatsheaf Public House, Thornton Heath:
'A Spirit Refreshed'

The first tells of a King (which King we don't know) who was travelling on the London Road with his daughter. As they were both tired and the hour late, they decided to pass the night at the "Wheatsheaf". For some unexplained reason, the daughter was taken ill and died in the night. However distressed the King may have been, his journey must have been of greater importance as he gave instructions for her body to be dumped in the conveniently adjacent pond. Annoyed at being so unceremoniously disposed of, her ghost, clad in a long white gown, is said to rise occasionally from the pond and enter the "Wheatsheaf" for "a quick half pint".

The other story is that the daughter of a landlord in a previous century was brutally murdered one night and her body thrown into the pond. She too is said to return for a drink whenever she feels the need, though I should imagine she could well have revenge on her mind.

Whether there is one ghost or two, they must have found life extremely uncomfortable when the pond was reduced in size some years ago and have probably ceased to exist altogether, now that it has been completely filled in. If either story is purely a work of fiction, it is surprising that the author has not come up with a highwayman or two, as the gallows stood opposite the pond and many a robber breathed his last on "Gallows Green".

Norbury is on the outskirts of Croydon and was mostly developed in the thirties but I considered it worthy of investigation. The library revealed nothing but the following story came to me through the post.

⚫

It is said that school days are the happiest days of one's life, but is this sufficient reason to haunt one's old school? Some people must think not, for the ghost that frequented **NORBURY MANOR BOYS' SCHOOL** in Stanford Road was considered to be that of somebody killed in a nearby air crash, or somebody who had died when the building was used as a military hospital in the First World War, rather than that of a former pupil. The school bell, which was situated in the most inaccessible part of the building, was supposed to ring for no explicable reason when the school was closed.

Although the ghost was never reported to have been seen, I like to think of him as a naughty schoolboy dared to climb to the roof by a fellow classmate. The school is now demolished, so that has put an end to his tricks, whoever he might have been.

Norbury is not particularly popular with the spiritual fraternity. There is, or was, the mystery of the boys school and I was told enigmatically of "something a short way North-east of the railway and police station". I thought there were no other tales until I heard of the strange events that occured in a flat above a workshop in the London Road.

The occupant had just been declared pregnant and was looking forward to the happy event. The cat however seemed less delighted. Usually a placid animal his behaviour became greatly disturbed. He would prowl about the rooms and took to scratching viciously at the bedroom and wardrobe doors. Wondering at the change in his temperament his owner came to the conclusion that the cat must be aware of a presence unknown to herself. She noticed a marked fall in the temperature of the usually cosy flat.

One evening she had to go out and requested a friend to stay whilst she was away as she had become frightened to return to an empty flat. She left him sitting in the lounge watching television and whilst he was doing so he suddenly felt as if some one had entered the room. Turning round slowly he saw what appeared to be a filmy white cloud. It remained for a few moments assuming strange but unrecognisable shapes then melted away leaving the room bitterly cold and the observer shaking. When the owner returned he told her what had happened and she said that he must have seen the ghost which she believed to be present.

The next day she told the story to the staff in the workshop below. Curious to know more they decided to take a reading both inside and outside the flat and to their astonishment they discovered that the temperature inside dropped to an abnormal level. Their interest further aroused, they arranged to enter the flat one at a time to see what they could experience for themselves. The first man to enter saw nothing but was exceptionally cold and was convinced of an unearthly presence whilst the second felt nothing and said it was mere imagination. The third man had just begun to ascend the stairs when he heard a door slam shut. Knowing the flat to be empty this made him very nervous and he returned to the workshop to ask the previous man to go with him as he had left the doors open. On examining the doors, they found that they could not have slammed of their own accord as new carpet had been laid and the bottoms needed to be shaved before they could move freely. They saw nothing, no floating cloud, even the cat had vacated the premises but they both descended the stairs shivering and the second man had second thoughts about it being "mere imagination".

CHAPTER III — NORWOOD

Not all ghosts are as elusive as those at Norbury. **ST JOSEPH'S COLLEGE** which stands on Beulah Hill, has been haunted by a very substantial ghost since 1864 and even today his presence is still felt.

St. Joseph's College, Norwood:
'Winners and Losers'

Until the college was bought in 1903 it was a private dwelling known as "The Grecian Villa". It was surrounded by woods and fields and the wealthy owner, a Mr Prior, bred fine racehorses. These horses were cared for by a man named Daniel Philpot who took great pride in himself and his work. He was particularly fond of a horse called "Gibson's Glory", giving him extra attention and grooming, to prepare him for the "Two Thousand

Guineas" race. So convinced was he that the horse would win, that he backed it with every penny he had. But the horse lost and Daniel Philpot was ruined.

Unable to face the humiliation, he decided there was only one thing to do. He went to the stable and took the rope used to tether 'Gibson's Glory" back to the villa. Nobody was about, the house quite empty. He climbed the stairs leading to his master's bedroom, known as the "Oak Room" and having tied one end of the rope to the balustrade, he took one last look at himself in the mirror above the mantlepiece, put his head through the noose and flung himself from the window. This was on the evening of September 8th, 1864, and his body was found by the postman next morning. An inquest was held, the verdict being "suicide while the mind was disturbed by financial worries".

Some weeks later, Mr Prior, sleeping in the Oak Room, awoke to find the atmosphere intensely cold and, glancing at the mantlepiece, he saw the tall figure of a man gazing into the mirror and yet there was no reflection. So shocked was he that he passed out and when he came to, the figure had gone. Fearful of seeing the apparition again, he moved to another room, but the ghost was seen by several of the servants all of whom left immediately.

When the house became a college, the Oak Room was given to a Brother Idas. He too, found the atmosphere bitterly cold and was unable to get to sleep. He would hear footsteps in the room and have an overwhelming urge to look in the mirror. Before long he asked to be moved and was transferred to another room leaving the Oak Room for unsuspecting guests.

Since then Daniel Philpot has been seen by many Brothers, all of whom have given the same description. It would seem that he visits at least every five years and he was due to put in an appearance in 1988. I wonder if he did?

⋰

In the grounds of the **VIRGO FIDELIS CONVENT** at Norwood there stands an interesting old building now used as the junior girls school. It was bought in 1775 as a home for the Earl of Bristol and his mistress Mrs Nesbitt. Formerly described as a cottage, the building was much extended and became a popular venue for Society including many politicians and even King George III who visited on numerous occasions.

The Earl died in 1779 leaving the property to Mrs Nesbitt who continued to entertain lavishly and became increasingly influential in political affairs. After her death it was sold to a Mr John Crowley who established the "Park Hotel" which remained a fashionable resort until 1848. A well-known figure in nineteenth century Norwood was the Reverend Montague Browne who recorded interesting notes about the area. He says that the name "Crowley" was written over the front door and that when the building was purchased by the nuns they were unable to eradicate it, however hard they tried. He felt this to be "uncanny" and to add to the mystery of the building with its hidden cupboards and dark passages. Although many alterations have been made, the "spooky" atmosphere remains and some girls have felt quite nervous when walking along the corridors.

Another tale told to me by one of the Sisters, concerned an elderly nun who had lived at the convent for many years. One night, whilst she was in bed, she dreamed or received a vision of the convents' founder, Mother St Mary. She urged the sister to hurry to the dormitory because it was on fire. Responding immediately, she arrived in time to extinguish the fire before any serious damage was done. No visions have been seen since but perhaps would re-appear should another emergency arise.

⚶

In close proximity to the convent, stands the now closed **NORWOOD HOSPITAL** once said to be haunted. Staff would see doors open slowly, pause just long enough to allow someone to pass through, then quietly close. Lights would come on, flicker slightly, then be extinguished without explanation. Two ghosts were believed to be in residence, that of a man whose presence was made apparent by a strong smell of tobacco and a woman who was recognised by her expensive perfume.

When speaking to a stranger one day, I mentioned the ghost of Croydon General. She looked interested and asked if I knew of any other hospitals that were haunted. I hesitated before mentioning Norwood, there seemed so little to say. However as soon as I said the name her eyes opened wide. "That's it, I'm off!" she exclaimed and started for the door. Anxious to know more, I tried to waylay her. "Did you work there?" I asked. "I certainly did", she replied, as she ran from the room and off down the corridor. I wonder who knows the whole story?

⚶

At the junction of Beulah Hill and Spa Hill there is the entrance to what was once the **BEULAH SPA**. The gatekeeper's lodge still remains. In the 1860's the Beulah Spa was a fashionable resort for the gentry who went there to take the waters and to indulge in a variety of pleasurable pursuits. It would therefore be a fitting place for the hauntings of crinolined ladies and top-hatted gentlemen, but not so the ghost of the present day "Beulah Spa" public house.

A lady who had once lived there with her parents, told me that the building was intended to be built as a complete circle, but its construction was interrupted by the outbreak of the Second World War, so it never became more than a semi-circle. The private accommodation was on the first floor, and due to the unusual shape, if you came out of one room you could not necessarily see the door to the next.

One evening, as she was leaving her bedroom, she saw what she thought was her father or brother walking between the lounge and the other bedrooms, but when she entered the lounge they were seated in front of the television. Jumping to the conclusion that they had a burglar, they all left the lounge to search but found no-one. On another occasion, a barmaid saw a man of the same description climb the stairs to the private apartment, leaving the gate at the top swinging open, but again nobody was found. Footsteps were often heard crossing the public bar, but the room was empty. Was this the ghost of a previous visitor to the pleasure grounds who had lost his way? I think not, for this one was described as wearing a brown jumper and slacks!

▲

"THE SYCAMORES" on Beulah Hill is reputed to be the oldest house in the district. The cellars date from 1690 and the main part of the building from 1780. The Belvedere tower was added in the early nineteenth century when it became fashionable to have far-reaching views of the surrounding countryside.

The house is thought to have been an inn offering a refuge for travellers journeying through the Great North Wood of Croydon. If legend is to be believed there is one person who found the inn less than hospitable, a man-servant who, it is said, was murdered in the hall.

In the 1860's "The Sycamores" was the home of the aforementioned Reverend Montague Browne who was the first curate of the nearby All Saints church. Later in life when writing his memoirs and referrring to the time when he was resident in Norwood, he said that **"THE YEWS"** which adjoined "The Sycamores" was believed to be haunted, a story however locally attributed to the fact that the building had been vacant for a long time. He makes no mention of having any ghostly encounters in his own house but a subsequent owner and her family reported strange experiences from the time when they lived there in the thirties. One Sunday afternoon, whilst indulging in a leisurely lunch, one of the sons who was a writer asked to be excused as he had a story to finish and he wanted to catch the afternoon post. He went into the adjoining study and was soon heard typing steadily. After a while the typing stopped and footsteps were heard going upstairs. Before they were heard to descend the typing recommenced. The family were mystified, so the father went to ask the son if at any time he had gone upstairs. He replied that he hadn't but he too had heard the footsteps and presumed it was one of the family.

Suspecting an intruder, they searched the premises but nobody was found.

A self-professed medium who visited the house about that time, said that she was aware of the presence of a benign spirit. The family agreed that the unseen visitor meant them no harm as they were never frightened.

The Sycamores, Beulah Hill:
'A ghost on guard'

In the 1940's, one of the sons had married and he and his wife rented the house from the parents. One night, when he was at a regimental reunion, his wife decided to retire to bed with a book. After a while she turned off the light and was about to settle down, when she heard what sounded like someone in stockinged feet creeping along the passage to the bedroom door. Thinking it must be her husband, she called out that there was no need for such stealth as she was still awake. The footsteps stopped but nobody entered. She turned on the light and watched the door but nothing happened. Deciding her imagination must be playing tricks, she thought she would read for a few more minutes, then she turned off the light for a second time. No sooner had she done so, than she heard the same footsteps, this time retreating along the passage, then the closing of the landing door. Bravely she got out of bed and went on a tour of the house, but it was empty, her husband had not returned.

After the war, the couple started to accommodate students and agreed they should not mention the occasional visitations for fear of frightening the youngsters. However it was not long before the students experienced the ghost for themselves, once again Sunday lunch was disturbed. As they all sat down at the dining table, one of the students said he could hear somebody moving about upstairs. They all stopped to listen and heard what sounded like furniture being pushed about. Two of the boys, eager to display their courage, rushed upstairs expecting to apprehend a burglar, but nobody was there and nothing had been disturbed.

In the early 1950's, an elderly aunt arrived for a prolonged stay. The lady of the house, went shopping taking her two children with her. When she returned she was surprised to find the front door open and a little doll's pram wedged across the bottom of the stairs. Fearing something must be radically wrong, she called to her Aunt who emerged from the study brandishing a poker. When she saw it was her niece, she put her finger to her lips and whispered that she believed some stranger to be in the house as she had heard them climb the stairs. When questioned about the open door and the pram in the dangerous position, she replied that sooner or later the person was sure to take fright, come hurtling down the stairs to escape through the door and in so doing would trip over the pram thus giving the old lady the opportunity to hit the intruder with a poker! A well-conceived plan by an old lady but she need not have worried, for when her niece, armed of course with the poker, went upstairs to investigate, nobody was there.

As the ghost only became active when a newcomer entered the house, the husband's theory was that it liked to 'vet' strangers who, once approved, were allowed to stay without further disturbance. Visitors often commented on the warm welcoming atmosphere as they stepped over the threshold and the family themselves always felt happy and secure within its walls. Could the ghost who obviously saw his role as their family protector be the benevolent spirit of the manservant who met his death in the hall so many years ago? Certainly it has not been heard of for some considerable time since the family left the house.

♠

I never fail to enjoy a walk around Norwood where the air is surprisingly fresh and there are some fine trees. Some of the Victorian edifices have an appearance sinister enough to invite all kinds of supernatural phenomena but the ghosts show a marked preference for the most decorative buildings. One such is **"BEULAH LODGE"** in Church Road. Its white walls, blue shuttered windows and the carved bargeboards, suggest a fairytale illustration.

Built in the early nineteenth century, it is said to have been used as a hunting lodge by William IV. It was visited by the Reverend Montague Browne who was most fascinated by the long garden full of large, old trees. He described them as forming an avenue with foliage so thick that they gave complete shade, even on the hottest day. He went on to describe a large stone cross that stood mid-way along the avenue, covered in ivy yet bearing no inscription. The base was decorated with impressions of a couple of hour glasses and geometric circles, whilst clinging to its surface, were the fossil remains of animal jaws. In front was a concrete-lined trough presumably meant for water. The gentleman in residence had no explanation for the unusual garden ornament, as the Reverend Browne suggested it may have been the grave of a rich gypsy, part of the group who lived at Gypsy Hill when the estate was called Bewley.

Having such a mysterious garden, it is not surprising that the house is said to have been haunted. The ghost was not of the wealthy gypsy as one might imagine, but of a little girl, aged three, who died, when she fell down a well in the centre of the house. Many a misty night her small figure was seen dancing lightly across the rooftop. When I went to the house myself, I heard children laughing but that was on a warm sunny afternoon and no-one knew of the little night visitor.

⚠

Standing near **ANERLEY HILL**, close to the site of the Crystal Palace, is a small cottage. When it was sold, the previous owner, told the purchaser that she believed the house to be haunted and proceeded to describe her experiences.

25

She said that on various occasions she had definitely heard footsteps walking about when she know the house to be empty apart from herself. One evening, as she was sitting in her living room, she heard the front door slam shut. She was quite startled as she knew the door to be locked and hers was the only key. She heard footsteps approaching along the corridor and expected someone to enter but instead they passed and climbed the stairs. Convinced it was a burglar, she armed herself with a heavy object and went up after him. There was no more sound and as she switched on the light no intruder was to be seen, neither was there any sign of disturbance.

If the incident was the reason for her decision to move, she did not say, but she was fortunate that it did not deter her prospective buyer who moved in quite happily giving no further thought to the mystery, that is, until it was suddenly brought to mind by the strange antics of her dog. She had just finished a meal and gone into the kitchen to wash up leaving her dog in the living room. No sooner had she started than the dog began to bark in a loud excited manner. Rushing in to see what was amiss, she was surprised to find he was leaping up as if somebody was in front of him. She tried to pacify him but his hair was standing on end and he was extremely agitated. She dragged him into the kitchen, but as she let go his collar, he rushed back and continued to bark and paw at the empty air. Eventually he calmed down and nothing so extraordinary ever happened again. Perhaps the ghost who had frequently visited the previous owner thought it best to vacate the premises after a hostile reception from the angry little dog.

Although ghosts are presumed to show preference for old buildings, they are by no means confined to such places.

With their supposed ability to pass through walls, it is obvious that they can go anywhere they choose.

⚠

A lady wrote to me of a ghost that she had encountered in a modern flat belonging to her son at **UPPER NORWOOD**; she had visited whilst he was out to do some cleaning for him. As she was bending down in the kitchen, she suddenly had the feeling that she was not alone. Had her son returned unexpectedly? She stood up and turning slowly, glanced into the hall. There to her amazement, she saw the figure of a lady dressed in a small grey cape and bonnet. As she waited, the figure moved slowly up the hall, then disappeared through the wall. It was then that she realised that the flat had become icy cold, she was shivering and when she looked down, saw that her arms were covered in goose pimples. No doubt she was relieved when her husband came to collect her and she took comfort in the fact that he believed her story.

Although the flat itself was modern it had been built on the site of a very old house, so the ghost could probably have been that of a previous occupant. Anxious not to upset her son, my correspondent refrained from telling him of the experience until he had moved elsewhere and although she had often though of the little old lady, she never re-appeared on subsequent visits.

⚠

Although **CRYSTAL PALACE LOW-LEVEL STATION** is situated some distance from the centre of Croydon, it is interesting in that it has some active and energetic ghosts.

27

Whilst knocking in keys to hold down the rails, a plate-layer was killed by a train. Since then, at all hours of the day and night, the sound of his hammering is to be heard coming from the tunnel where the accident occured. Plate-laying being a hazardous occupation, it is hardly surprising that another workman suffered a similar fate. This poor unfortunate was decapitated and his headless figure has been seen wandering in the tunnel between Crystal Palace and Gypsy Hill.

One chargehand described the whole station as being "spooky", as he often heard strange unidentifiable noises at night. When alone in the staff office, he would lock himself in for greater security. Men in the old signal box, repeatedly heard heavy footsteps ascending the wooden staircase but nobody entered. This happened so often that they developed the custom of making a special brew whenever they were having tea themselves, and then flinging it from the window to ward off evil spirits. This must have been a very powerful potion for the haunting eventually ceased.

CHAPTER IV — SOUTH AND EAST

During my search in Croydon reference library, I came across a book on railway ghosts and was pleased to read of paranormal manoeuvrings at **ADDISCOMBE RAILWAY SHEDS.**

The sheds are used to clean and store carriages which are in service during the peak hours. They are consequently only empty in the mornings and evenings. It is said that during the night, cleaners trolleys are rarely where they have been left but are moved from place to place by unseen hands; that carriage doors are heard to open and close of their own accord. Even the trains have been heard trundling along the rails inside the sheds yet found to be in their original positions on inspection.

There have been several accidents on the site, one in which a boiler exploded killing four people, another when a train ran through the end of a shed killing the driver and a blacksmith whose smithy was unfortunately situated behind the building, and one in which a shunter was crushed between two carriages in number four shed. This area is always described as being particularly cold so the spirit of the shunter is thought to be responsible for the night-time trickery. Various staff are said to have seen the shunter leaving the sheds or walking on the tracks. He is described as being a grey misty figure of indeterminate outline and having a white face with blurred features.

Being intrigued by this comparatively modern apparition, I visited the station to ask the staff how familiar they were with their legendary colleague, how very disappointed I was. Yes, they had heard the stories, but neither they nor anybody they know had had the doubtful pleasure of the shunter's company. They did admit to the sheds being very eerie at night and to number four shed being exceedingly cold, but that was all. As I was about to leave I was issued with an invitation to spend the night if I wished, just in case something should turn up, but I found it an invitation I could easily refuse.

⚛

Whilst researching this book I was called to a Croydon hospital for a routine check-up. When giving the receptionist the usual details, she asked my occupation. When I told her I was writing a book about ghosts, she became extremely excited and asked if she could visit me at home. I agreed and we arranged a date.

When the day came she arrived clutching a small folder, the contents of which she promised to show me later. She said that since moving into her flat in the **CROHAM HURST** area, she had been convinced of some spiritual presence. The house built in the Victorian era, was falling into gentle decay and had its own aura, but the garden was even more atmospheric.

From the folder she produced some black and white photographs and presented them to me one by one. The first was of a derelict greenhouse containing a collection of old junk draped in ragged dust sheets. The next was a tangle of branches showing years of growth and neglect. Staring hard into the photograph I was sure I could see the face of a bat, but she just smiled. The third was of flowers, long grass and twisted iron. I could see nothing of significance at first, but on looking more closely, I suddenly saw the face of a child. It was a girl with light-coloured hair and round chubby cheeks gazing sadly from the foliage. When I said what I could see, my visitor produced an enlarged copy, which not only showed the face distinctly, but an accompanying face that appeared to be wearing a mask similar to those worn at a fancy dress ball. I found the pictures quite fascinating and could understand why they added to her conviction that the house was haunted.

Personally I remained rather sceptical until I received a letter from a gentleman once resident in Caterham. He told me that some years ago twin babies living in the district had died and when a photograph was taken of the flowers on the grave, the babies' faces were clearly seen among the foliage. It gave me cause to reconsider; perhaps the eye of the camera is more sensitive to ghosts than we are ourselves. Maybe the little blond girl and her masked partner did live and die in Croham Hurst.

⚶

A ghost that made its presence felt whilst remaining totally invisible was an unforgetable experience for a gentleman living in South Croydon. On returning from an evening out, he and a friend decided to take a short cut to his home by walking through **LLOYD PARK**. It was quite dark but with the help of the street lights they were able to see the way ahead. They had not gone far before their attention was caught by some strange marks on the grass. A closer inspection revealed it to be a complete circle with what looked like symbols placed around the edges at regular intervals. Their first thought was that somebody had been dabbling in the occult and they looked around apprehensively. Then the friend had a

31

different idea, he had once trained to be a park keeper and it occurred to him that the marks could have been caused by some heavy machinery used in park maintenance. Relieved at this explanation, they laughed at their previous notion and walked on.

They were only about thirty yards further along the path when one of the men was overcome by what he felt to be an overpowering feeling of menace. The atmosphere was sinister and threatening. He looked around nervously, lights glowed comfortably in the houses across the park and the street lights threw patterns of orange and black across the grass. Nothing else was to be seen but he was convinced that something evil was very near. He wanted to speak to his companion but he couldn't, he wanted to scream out a prayer but the muscles tightened in his throat and no sound emerged; all he could do was keep walking straight ahead, never looking to left or right until the park gates loomed up before him. He staggered through gasping for breath and turning saw his friend pale and shaken beside him. For a few seconds they just stared at each other, then the friend said "What *was* that?" Neither could answer but both knew they had suffered the same experience.

When as members of the Christian Church, they attended a seminar, they decided it was a good opportunity to relate the terrifying episode to one of the lecturers. He listened with interest and said that such experiences were not uncommon and the cause was usually attributed to a ghoul. According to my dictionary, a ghoul is a spirit that preys on corpses so what was it doing in Lloyd Park? Would investigations reveal a body or even an ancient burial ground beneath those pleasant grassy slopes?

Not far from Lloyd Park, on the corner of **CONDUIT LANE**, is a pond best avoided, particularly around midnight. There were once three conduits here, two supplying water to Coombe House and the other supplying Coombe Lodge. The water then ran into a pond situated next to the lodge. In the early 1860s local residents often told of the phantom of a young servant girl standing by the pool. In 1845 the pond was filled in and a new one was made at the corner of Conduits Lane. Was this the end of the servant girl's wanderings? Not at all; completely undeterred she made the new pool her nightly venue. Perhaps she was a little angry at the change of situation though, because one night she is reported to have knocked the helmet off the head of the local police constable! The pond, which was formerly called "Brown's, has now been enclosed.

CHAPTER V — ADDINGTON

Coombe Lane eventually leads to Gravel Hill where **ADDINGTON PALACE** now houses the Royal School of Church Music. Originally called Addington Place, it was re-named in 1807 when it was sold under an Act of Parliament to the Archbishop of Canterbury. Apparently the area around the Old Palace in Croydon had become unhealthy, due to the many ponds surrounding it, and the streams which became open sewers as the population of Croydon grew.

Six Archbishops lived there, but only the last, Edward Benson, has deemed the palace worthy of haunting. Why does he return to wander along the corridors? Does he really visit his old home or it is just a trick of some choirboys' imagination? For I have it on good authority that they are the only people to have made his acquaintance.

The very name **"NEW" ADDINGTON** would suggest an absence of ghosts but I found two in the area. One is said to be of a German pilot who was killed when he bailed out of his plane during an air battle over Addington in World War II.

Some years later, a man walking in **QUEEN ELIZABETH'S DRIVE** realised he had lost his wallet, so retraced his steps in an effort to find it. Suddenly a fair haired young man wearing a leather flying jacket appeared in front of him. Speaking in a foreign accent, he asked the startled man if he had lost a wallet and when he replied that he had it was handed to him. Greatly relieved at seeing his property again, the man started to thank the pilot but he had gone.

Not far away from Queen Elizabeth's Drive can be found a very different ghost, that of "Digger Harry". His haunt is **BEARE'S WOOD**, off Courtwood Lane, now used as a scout camp. In the 1800s, a small cottage stood among the trees and was occupied by Harry and his wife, where they lived in complete domestic bliss. One day much to Harry's distress, his beloved wife died. Knowing that, if he reported it, her body would be taken away and placed in a cemetery, thus parting them, he decided to say nothing. Instead he buried her in the woods she loved so much.

Some time later her absence was noticed and the police arrested Harry for murder. He was put into prison, but released six months later because of his old age. He returned to his cottage, but could not remember where he had buried his loved one. Completely heartbroken and desperately lonely he soon died.

Though his body was lain to rest, his spirit was not. First seen in 1932, his ghost now wanders through the woods, shovel in hand, still searching for his wife's grave. What a delightful story for the boy scouts to tell as they sit around the dying embers of their camp fire!

CHAPTER VI — CROYDON AIRPORT

Some distance from Croydon, where the traffic thunders along the Purley Way, stands the old **CROYDON AIRPORT**. When it opened in 1915 the Airport was a busy centre of activity. Used for training purposes to begin with, it later became the airport for London. From 1939 it was used as a fighter base until the end of World War II when it re-opened for civil purposes. It survived until 1959 when it finally closed as it was too small for modern aircraft.

Having been used by so many people for such a variety of reasons, it is not surprising that some of them have returned in spirit form. As far as I can gather, the first to arrive was the ghost of a Dutch pilot in the 1930s. He died when his plane crashed in fog after taking off from Croydon following a favourable but grossly incorrect weather report. About a fortnight later, a pilot of Imperial Airways, was plotting his flight course when a voice behind him said, "You can't take off, the weather is just the same as when I did". Knowing himself to be alone in the room, the pilot was startled and spun around to find the figure of the dead pilot wearing his flying kit, standing behind him. The British pilot was still in a state of shock when found by a colleague soon after. Although the sky was quite clear, it was deemed best to cancel the flight and later a thick fog descended as the Dutch airman had predicted.

⁂

There is very little of the original airfield left as the main part is now covered by the **ROUNDSHAW** estate. This has not deterred the departed souls. In 1971, when the estate was being constructed, some council workmen, engaged in their labours, were disturbed by the sound of a motorbike coming towards them. Looking up, they saw a cyclist clad in battle dress tear round the boiler house then dash past them at high speed. They were horrified, for although the rider wore a helmet, as he looked back at them, they saw that he had no face. Local legend suggests it to have been the ghost of a Battle of Britain airman who was killed when his plane crashed at the end of the runway.

This same ghost was also seen by two residents of Roundshaw when they were driving along **MOLLISON DRIVE** at about 2 a.m. They were suddenly forced to swerve in order to avoid hitting the motor-cyclist who was tearing along at full speed although no sound came from the engine. The 'Wallington Times' of October 1979 reported the ghost to have been exorcised, which must have been a great relief to all concerned.

▲

It would seem that ghosts are particularly antagonistic towards workmen, probably because they do not like their habitats disturbed, for another group of men suffered from spiritual interruption. They were sleeping on the site at the time and were woken one night by the sound of community singing. Pondering on what it could be they came to the conclusion that it was either the ethereal voices of R.A.F. personnel at a N.A.A.F.I. concert or singing from an air raid shelter whilst the occupants waited for the all-clear. Another theory was that they could be voices of the sixty people who were killed during an air attack on the airport in 1940 which struck the

Bourjois Perfume Factory. This was the first air raid of the War on Metropolitan London and its circumstances are still shrouded in official mystery some 50 years later. Regretfully in reporting the incident, the workmen failed to name the tunes, to have done so might have provided a clue to the singers identity.

Croydon Airport, The Central Tower:
'Voices in the ether?'

The council workmen must have been quite stout hearted as they weren't intimidated by the spirits and the estate was finished; but the many tons of concrete failed to lay the ghosts. In 1975 and 1976 the ghosts of three nuns were seen on the walkways of Roundshaw. One lady saw them so often that she felt compelled to move house. The description given of their garments were identical to those worn by three nuns killed on the runway in January 1947. The aircraft in which they had been travelling was caught in a snowstorm and crashed, busting into flames.

Twelve people were burned to death as they struggled to escape. One of the nuns must have had a premonition, because she told a friend before leaving, that if she did not finish her journey on earth she would finish it in heaven.

⁜

AIRPORT HOUSE as it now stands, is subject to a preservation order. It presents a sad face to the world, gone are it's days of glory, yet it still manages to maintain that vital element, atmosphere. It is now used as offices by a wide variety of businesses and I worked there myself for a short period. On one occasion I had the opportunity to climb to the control tower. The square glass room was completely empty except for the sad little body of a thrush that must have entered through a broken window. As I gazed across the remaining strip of green field, I found it easy to imagine the thrills and excitement of those early years. It did not surprise me in the least to read somewhere that a caretaker going about the building late at night, had heard voices in the conference room, for I heard them too, in the control tower.

On a site so rich in history where there have been many events of an exciting or tragic nature, to walk in the gathering gloom at the end of a winter's afternoon is to invite a confrontation with many a departed spirit.

Further afield there is a tall, red brick, mansion, once the home of the Carew family. Previously called Beddington Park, it is now re-named **CAREW MANOR**. It has undergone many changes since it was built and little of the original structure remains. Now in use as a school it was a girls' orphanage from 1866 until 1939.

The Carews were wealthy landowners and a very distinguished family. In 1592, the daughter of Sir Francis Carew, Elizabeth Throckmorton, was married to Sir Walter Raleigh. At the time she was a maid of honour to Queen Elizabeth I who was so displeased with the marriage that she had Walter Raleigh imprisoned for some time. This did nothing to destroy their affection for each other, for when Raleigh was beheaded in Old Palace yard in 1618, his grieving widow had his head placed in a leather bag which she is said to have carried with her for the rest of her life. His body was quietly removed and taken to **BEDDINGTON** for a secret burial in the churchyard.

A story handed down over the centuries, says that **RALEIGH'S GHOST** haunts the walk behind the old Yew tree. Apparently a student of psychical research spent two nights on the walk but saw nothing in spite of being aware of a definite presence. What a disappointment for the student, who was probably looking forward to a colourful spectacle of the traditional Elizabethan head-under-arm ghost!

Though he saw nothing of Sir Walter, a gentleman from South Croydon did have a strange experience in this Beddington churchyard. Whilst researching the history of Beddington and its connections with Raleigh, he was

40

walking among the tombstones when he came across a mass grave of young girls who had died in an epidemic which broke out when the manor was in use as an orphanage. Out of curiousity he took a photograph which when developed showed a grey mist hovering over the grave. Although the picture was one of thirty-six exposures, no other photograph was similarly affected. Whether the mist had any particular shape or colour he did not say but he could think of no satisfactory explanation.

Beddington Parish Church:
'Knight errant'

Not far from Carew Manor stands **ST PHILOMENA'S** girls' school. An elegant Queen Anne mansion, it started out as Carshalton House and stands on the corner of Pound Street surrounded by a high red brick wall. Originally a private dwelling, it was built by Edward Carleton who bankrupted himself and was forced to sell the house in 1713 to a Dr. John Radcliffe who was the Royal physician. The doctor soon regretted his purchase as the distance from London was too far, especially in an emergency. Such an emergency did arise when the Queen had a particularly bad attack of gout. She sent a messenger to collect him but, angry at being summoned, the doctor flew into a rage and threw the messenger down the stairs breaking his neck. Soon after, the ghost of the dead man returned to haunt the staircase. This was too much for the doctor. He became increasingly depressed, his health deterioriated and he died.

The next purchaser was a gentleman by the name of John Fellows, who was later knighted. Misfortune soon befell him, in that he lost all his money in the South Sea Bubble of 1720. He soon received a call from the tax collector which so enraged him that he too threw his visitor down the stairs causing yet another broken neck. The tax collector also returned to haunt the staircase. One cannot help but wonder if the ghosts formed a liaison or arranged some form of rota.

The stairs were not the only part of the house to be haunted if legend is to be believed. A butler is said to have murdered a housemaid and nightly their ghosts gave a lively re-enactment of the scene in the **LONG GALLERY**. When the house became a Convent, strange noises were heard so often that one of the sisters decided to investigate. Taking some companions for support, she crept into the Long Gallery and there they witnessed the whole horrendous performance. As a result of this experience an exorcist was called in who successfully put paid to the activities.

Three murders would seem enough for one house but yet another is said to have taken place there. This time the victim was the gardener's boy, though whether the gardener was the culprit or not the story does not say. Apparently a nun who was a novice at the time, had gone to her bedroom which was a cubicle leading off a larger room at the top of the house. She was feeling unwell and was soon asleep. At about midnight she was woken by a loud noise outside the door. Thinking it to be a prank by some of the other novices, she went out to ask them to quieten down. She expected the light to be on, but the room was in pitch darkness. As she stood petrified, she heard scuffling then a dull thud and something heavy being dragged across the floor. The room became quiet except for a sharp rasping sound as if someone was trying to get their breath. Then the dragging sound began again ending only when the door on the other side of the room opened and closed. When she reported the incident she was told that a man strangled the gardener's boy on the top floor of the house and dragged his body into the next room where he deposited it in a packing case before hammering down the lid. The hammering is still supposed to be heard.

CHAPTER VIII — PURLEY AND COULSDON

Along the Brighton Road, just before the town centre of Purley, there stands the **'ROYAL OAK'** public house which purports to have a well-respected ghost.

The present building is on a site slightly removed from the original one and it is in the lounge bar that the visitor seems most comfortable. Various members of staff have made his acquaintance. He is described as being an elderly man who walks with a stoop and leans heavily on a stick. He scares nobody because his expression is friendly and when he is present a feeling of warmth pervades the atmosphere.

Local customers have said that a small timber yard and market garden once stood on the site, and that the gentleman who owned it was extremely good-natured and offered hospitality to the staff of the nearby tram depot, serving them refreshments whenever required. Assuming the ghost to be that of the old market gardener, he probably misses the jolly camaraderie of the tram drivers, long since gone, so he chooses to seek companionship in the comfort of the local public house that replaces his business and his old home.

⚕

I was disappointed to find only one other ghost story in Purley. I am sure there must be more but so far they have eluded me. This story was told to me by a lady who was working as an agency nurse at the time. She was sent to a house in Purley where she was given the responsibility of caring for an elderly gentleman who was suffering from Parkinson's Disease and needed constant attention.

44

As she approached the once immaculate 1920s house she felt a strange sense of foreboding. It was dismal and depressing and looked as if it had had no attention since the day it was built. She was admitted by the lady of the house who appeared to be very nervous and highly strung. The patient was bedridden and sat propped up against a mound of pillows in a dark, stuffy room. The nurse's first duty was to give him supper and she was curious to notice that he appeared to be sharing his meal with some invisible person. His wife fussed around treating him as a baby and at the end of the evening whispered to the nurse that she would be sleeping in a room across the landing if she was required.

After settling the patient for the night, the nurse sat in a chair beside the bed and started to read a book. She must have fallen asleep as she woke with a start some time later feeling intensely cold and shivering from head to toe. She drew her chair closer to the fire but although she could feel the heat burning her legs she continued to shiver. Thinking a hot drink might help, she crept from the room, closing the door tightly behind her. When she returned she was surprised to find it wide open.

The next night at precisely the same time, she again felt a terrible blast of cold air. She resisted the urge to go downstairs but wrapped herself in a duvet and huddled against the bed in a chair facing the door. She tried to remain awake but was eventually overcome with tiredness and fell asleep once again. How long for she did not know, but woke suddenly with the feeling that someone was clutching at her throat. She rose from the chair, coughing and choking, hardly able to breathe. She staggered to the door and wrenching it open almost fell onto the landing. As she attempted to recover her breath she heard voices coming from below; looking over the bannisters she was surprised to see three little girls in smock dresses playing in the hallway. Wondering at their appearance and deciding they could hardly be responsible for her near strangulation, she walked slowly downstairs. The children continued to play but as she reached the last stair they vanished. Thinking it might just have been a dream she made a cup of coffee and returned to the bedroom. She went in cautiously, fearful that her attacker might still be present but all was quiet, the old man slept peacefully and the cold air seemed to have dispersed.

When she told a neighbour of the bizarre events, she said she was not surprised; the old man had previously had two resident nurses one of whom had left hurriedly without explanation and another who had suffered a heart-attack. It was said that the paperboy no longer went up to the house but threw the paper over the hedge as he had once seen an apparition. Reporting back to the agency, the nurse asked for another assignment.

Two years later she was working in a nursing home instructing a newcomer on night duties. At breaktime they both went to a vacant room where the girl, who was evidently psychic, was seen to shiver and asked if anyone had died there. She was told that it was possible that somebody had, whereupon she started to relate a nasty experience she had had when working in a private house. She described the same choking sensation that had affected the first nurse. When asked where this had occurred, it was, of course the same address. The first nurse was surprised to receive further corroboration of her own and the girl's experience from a third nurse who at the same house similarly had heard a loud rustling noise and felt a rush of cold air which she considered to be the passage of the evil spirits but as she was wearing a crucifix at the time presumed this had protected her from coming to any harm.

⚛

Beyond Purley and high on a hill is **OLD COULSDON**. Now a pleasant but typical Croydon suburb its heart is preserved in the Bradmore Green conservation area. Beside the wide Green, stands the picturesque old church of **ST. JOHN** and close by is the Grange, once the courthouse where local inhabitants were tried for their misdemeanours.

Some twenty years ago and at about eight o'clock in the morning, a gardener was attending to his work in the churchyard. As he was bending over a grave he suddenly felt compelled to look up; to his amazement he saw a figure wearing a long black cloak standing by the far wall. Though surprised by his appearance the gardener presumed it was a stranger searching perhaps, for a relative's grave. He left his work and started to walk over to see if he could be of assistance but before he reached him the figure had vanished. Thinking the man must have jumped over the wall he ran to look but there was no-one in sight. It was then that he realised that in spite of his exertions he was feeling unnaturally cold and his hands were shaking. He returned to his work but spent the rest of the day pondering on the strange event of the morning and giving many a nervous glance towards the wall in case the stranger should return.

He told his wife of the uncanny experience but she seemed to think it of little consequence and as time went

47

by the incident was forgotten. Then one day, noting that the grass was beginning to get out of hand in the churchyard, he asked his youngest son if he would like to earn some extra pocket money by giving him some help. His offer was eagerly accepted and they set off together each taking a separate part of the graveyard. Hardly had work commenced, than the boy went running over to his Father to say that he had seen a strange figure in a long black cloak standing by the wall, but of course there was nobody there when they returned to the spot.

St. John's Church, Old Coulsdon:
'Stranger in long black cloak'

Though the figure never returned again to the gardener he did have another frightening experience. He had occasion to enter the church and as he was walking up one side of the aisle he was aware of footsteps going up the other side although he appeared to be alone. Once again he felt bitterly cold and was trembling as he had been on the previous encounter. When he mentioned the unidentified footsteps to the curate he said that he had heard them too.

By delving into the various books I have recording Coulsdon's history I hoped to be able to identify the mysterious visitor but although I found some clear descriptions of previous inhabitants, I failed to discover the man in black. Perhaps you, reading this, know who he was, or has he passed completely out of living memory?

CHAPTER IX — KENLEY

Although many more houses are springing up among the trees, **KENLEY** is still one of the more rural outposts of Croydon.

On the left hand side of the Godstone Road as you travel towards Caterham, there is an ancient strip of downland known as Riddlesdown. In the late eighteenth century, a chalk track that proceeds across the crest of the hill was the old road from London to Lewes and it descends to join the Godstone Road by a deserted chalk quarry.

On the opposite side of the road is a public house called the **"ROSE AND CROWN"**. The present building is the third to be built on the site, the original one being a coaching inn and much favoured as a refreshment stop by travellers on the journey south. Legend has it that there was once a serious accident at this spot; a coach and horses went out of control on the steep downward slope and crashed opposite the inn. Since then, various local people, have reported seeing a large black coach pulled by four horses, come hurtling down the track only to vanish the instant it has reached the main road.

⚜

Not strictly a ghost story but an interesting one nevertheless is the one from **WELCOMES FARM** in Hayes Lane.

Once used as a racing stable the building became derelict when the owner died. After the war it was purchased for the same purpose by a man called Dyer who had placed all his gratuity money on the winner of the Lincolnshire

Handicap. In this business venture, he took as a partner Eric Tombe, another horse racing enthusiast, who was a son of an Oxfordshire vicar. It was not long before it became obvious that the partnership was a great mistake, arguments ensued and Eric Tombe mysteriously disappeared. The police were called in and although they were suspicious of Dyer they could find no incriminating evidence. Some time later the farm was destroyed by fire and once again suspicion fell on Dyer but there was no positive proof of his guilt. The police carried out further investigations into Dyer's affairs and found him guilty of stealing from the farm accounts by forging the signature of Eric Tombe on a number of cheques. Not surprisingly, it was found that Dyer had also disappeared, so an intensive search was mounted and he was traced to a hotel in Scarborough. Realising he was trapped when the police moved in, Dyer produced a gun and during a violent struggle he shot himself.

About a year later, Eric Tombe's mother had a vivid dream in which she saw the body of her son lying at the bottom of a well. Her husband reported this to the police who descended in full force on Welcomes Farm. The stables and yard were in a ruinous state, the charred remains of the farmhouse overgrown with weeds making the search for a well a formidable task. By the time it was discovered night had fallen and it was necessary to shine lamps down into the murky depths. The lights revealed a decomposing body which when it was hauled to the surface proved to be that of Eric Tombe. He was identified by the watch he was wearing and various other personal belongings which Dyer had disposed of knowing he would be incriminated if they were found in his possession. This story would appear to be a clear indication that it is possible for the spirit of a dead human being to penetrate the subconscious of a living one.

♨

OLD LODGE LANE winds its exceedingly narrow way up the hill from Purley to Kenley It is a quiet lane overhung with trees, at its busiest when it is closing time at the **WATTENDEN ARMS**.

Not far from the 'Wattenden', on the opposite side of the road is the site of what was once **GARSTON HALL**. It was severly damaged in World War II and subsequently demolished. When clearing the debris, workmen located the remains of an old tunnel leading to "Barn cottages" in Hayes Lane. It has been suggested that the tunnel belonged to an earlier building which some believe to have been a convent but this is pure conjecture. Garston Hall was owned by the Byron family who owned much of the land in the area. It was used as a kennels for the breeding and training of the famous "Old Surrey" foxhounds. Facing the site is a row of cottages built to house the groomsmen.

A young girl living in one of the cottages was convinced it was haunted as she often heard footsteps going about the house when she knew herself to be alone in the building. She told her Father who refused to take it seriously, that is, until he too had a strange experience. Standing in his living room on a bright summer's day, he suddenly had the feeling that someone was watching him. He felt very cold and as he turned round his hair stood on end, for in the doorway stood the figure of a tall, broad-shouldered man dressed in a dark old-fashioned suit and wearing a wing-collar. The figure remained there for a few minutes then as the father watched, it seemed to gradually dissolve. When he had had a chance to recover the father decided it must have been the ghost of a groomsman who had once occupied the house and whose footsteps had been disturbing his daughter for so long.

Quite shaken by the incident, he waited anxiously for his daughter's return. When she arrived he recounted the afternoons events to her and she was glad to know that he now believed her story. They wondered what it was he had wanted and whether he would return, but he was never seen again.

⩜

Without doubt the most renowned ghost of Kenley is that of the "GREY LADY", familiar as she is to the local folk and those living farther afield.

I first heard of her when researching the local architecture. When talking to residents, she would frequently drift, as it were into the conversation. Though not particularly interested in ghosts at the time, it was difficult to ignore the possibility of her existence; especially when walking along narrow lanes as dusk was falling.

The figure is generally supposed to be that of a nun sometimes carrying a bundle in her arms that resembles a baby. In 1966 when the Bourne Society were excavating in Hayes Lane to find the lost village of Watendone, they unearthed human bones and the foundations of an old chapel known to have burned down in 1780. It is from this site that the lady is supposed to begin her wanderings.

A young lady told me that she was walking in Hayes Lane near the junction with Firs Road, when a lady wearing a long grey cloak appeared as if from nowhere. She recognised the figure to be not of this world but was not frightened because of the gentle, rather sad expression on her face. Almost as soon as she arrived she vanished leaving nothing but a faint smell of flowers.

When she got home she told her mother who laughed and said it must be a figment of her imagination, but she apologised later when she heard that other people had had similar experiences.

Further up the lane there is a house where a previous owner was said to have heard her baby screaming and hurrying into the bedroom saw the shadowy figure of a woman leaning over the cot. As she rushed forward the woman disappeared.

At the top of the lane in another dwelling the 'Grey Lady' seems to have been a frequent visitor. She was seen by the owner to be standing under a tree in the garden and terrified the maid, who, on seeing a figure sitting in a garden chair presumed it was her mistress and had gone to speak to her only to have the apparition vanish in front of her. The daughter-in-law told me that when she went down stairs one morning she saw the 'Grey Lady' standing in the hall. As she approached the 'lady' passed straight through the dining room door though it remained closed. A neighbour reported having seen the figure in the garden under a cedar tree; she called out a friendly greeting but the 'Grey Lady' faded away.

Welcomes Road with its many trees and pleasant houses has also been one of her favourite haunts. A motorist returning from work, is said to have found her standing on his driveway. When he got out of his car to ask her to move she is supposed to have melted into the hedge. One gentleman told me that he was walking up the road one winter evening when a strange apparition appeared before him. The shape was indistinct but surrounded by a blue aura and he smelt very sweet perfume. As he advanced up the road the luminescent shape floated ahead of him until it vanished at the junction with Uplands Road.

Perhaps the ghost goes into houses in the area, as I have heard from a previous resident that when living in a house there he and his wife often felt they were not alone and that their Siamese cats behaved as if strangers were present. Although they were not disturbed by the unseen presence, a visitor who came to stay, repeatedly heard crying on the staircase and felt the ghost to be in great distress. In other houses residents have heard unexplained knocks at the windows and mysterious footsteps.

In the garden of a house in Welcomes Road, an ancient altar was found which contributed to the belief of some that there had been a monastery in the vicinity and that the house had been built on what was once a monks' walk. There is said to have been a smell of candle grease and perfume. Behind the houses there is a wood which hides the remains of an old flint and brick building; one gentleman described it as being a sort of cave with a brick arch in front. It is supposed to have been inhabited by a hermit, an idea supported by the close proximity of Hermitage Road, but could it also have some connection with the 'Grey Lady'?

A more recent incident involving Kenley's favourite ghost, was that experienced by the estate manager at **KENLEY HOUSE.** He was working in his office, when one of the cleaners entered and said there was a lady waiting by the greenhouse presumably to see him. Leaving the building he went outside to greet the visitor but when he reached the greenhouse nobody was there. He then went to find the cleaner and asked what the lady had looked like. She replied that she was unusually dressed in a long grey cloak. When he explained to the cleaner that she must have seen the "Grey Lady" she was astonished as she had never heard the story before, probably due to the fact that she did not live in that area.

Kenley House, Kenley:
'The Grey Lady of Kenley'

Although he has never seen any such figure himself, the

manager has repeatedly felt a strange presence on the top floor of Kenley House were the nursery was once situated. Each time it has caused him to break out in a cold sweat and his hair to stand on end. Perhaps the "Grey Lady" searches there for the baby sometimes seen as a bundle cradled in her arms.

When the house was completely renovated in 1981, an old, very deep well was found. It had belonged to Kenley Farm which stood on the site in the eighteenth century. Rumour has it that a stable lad was flung down there for misbehaving and that he has been haunting the house ever since. If this is so, he has not introduced himself to the manager — as yet.

It was a bright Autumn morning when I last walked up Welcomes Road, not on the trail of the 'Grey Lady' this time but to visit a house reputed to be haunted by a child. The sun streamed through the yellowing leaves of the trees and their trunks cast long black shadows across the ground. Although only eleven o'clock in the morning, there was already a definite air of mystery. This was further enhanced by the wide-eyed stare I received from a black cat and the strange antics of a scruffy dog who, having appeared from nowhere, proceeded to circle round me whining as he did so and glaring balefully at me from the corner of his eyes. I was much relieved when something distracted his attention and he ran off.

When I found the house I was looking for and explained the reason for my visit, the owner smiled knowingly and invited me in. He said that although he had had no unpleasant experiences in his home, he knew it was rumoured to be haunted and was interested to know what I had been told. I then proceeded to divulge the information given to be by a previous resident, a lady.

She said that when she and her husband first visited the house with the estate agent, it had been a warm sunny day in June, but that the house had felt intensely cold. She wanted to leave at once, but as the building was of a most attractive appearance, and contained exactly the accommodation they required, she dismissed her fears as being quite irrational, and they agreed to purchase.

No sooner had they moved in than the trouble began. One morning as the lady was sitting on the bed, a large pane of glass from the double glazing, fell from the window and smashed to pieces, missing her by inches. They had it replaced by an expert but within a few days it happened again. Breakages became common place, they would often come down in the morning to find valuable items lying in fragmented heaps on the floor.

One night, when in bed, they thought they heard their child crying in the next room, but when they went to see what troubled him he was fast asleep. No sooner had they returned to bed and settled down again than they heard little footsteps pattering across the landing. Convinced that the child was out of bed, they went to put him back, but he was still in his cot, the covers firmly tucked in. This became a common occurence and caused them many sleepless nights. Visitors to the house also heard the child crying and were always surprised to find him quite well in the mornings.

One evening, as they were sitting in their living room, what sounded and felt like a violent gust of wind surged across the room pinning the heavy velvet curtains to the windows where they stayed for a few minutes until the wind subsided, then they fell back into place. They went all round the house searching for an open door or window, something that could have caused the draught, but found nothing. Later that evening, the lady went up to have a bath. When she had finished she realised there was no towel. Thinking she could hear her husband outside the bathroom door, she called to him to bring her one from the airing cupboard but there was no response. Wrapping herself in some clothing she went downstairs to find him sitting in front of the television where he insisted he had been the whole time.

The next mystery occurred in the study where a dark red stain resembling blood appeared on the wall over-night. It was wet and sticky and difficult to remove. Although they eventually succeeded, it was there again next morning. This happened so often that they decided to cover it with very thick paper, but still it crept through. Utterly exhausted by the whole business and considering moving the lady spoke to her next door neighbour who said that the house had had many owners all of whom had experienced great unhappiness. One had even called in an exorcist in the hope of leading a more peaceful life, but to no avail.

Still hoping to find some solution, they then called in a medium. She said that she could see a little girl running from room to room as if desperately seeking a way out and suggested they opened the front door to enable her to escape. Feeling rather foolish, the lady did as she was told and as she did so she felt something brush against her leg as it passed.

From that moment the disturbances ceased and they wondered whether to reverse their decision to move but as they had already set the wheels in motion, they decided to go ahead and put the house on the market.

They were pleased to find many people came to view but none returned after the first visit. This continued for a year until they came to the conclusion that the potential buyers must be experiencing the same deathly chill that had first affected them. They decided to call in the local priest who effected an exorcism. Imagine their delight when they found a purchaser the very next day.

The present owner listened with interest throughout and when I had finished he got up without speaking and smilingly led me to the study; in the corner of the room was a dark red stain, still there after many years. We exchanged glances then agreed it was probably caused by condensation, at least we hoped it was. As we returned to the living room he was called away to the telephone.

I gazed out of the window to where a sunny lawn, spotted with brown and yellow leaves sloped upwards. A squirrel scrabbled about and a colourful jay perched on a convenient branch. It was all very peaceful, like a garden of rest, and I wondered, could this be where the "Grey Lady's" baby had died and was buried? and could this be the reason for her frequent visits to Welcomes Road?

CHAPTER X — CATERHAM

Caterham consists of two lively communities, one on the hill and the other in the valley. Although it maintains an air of independance, I think it can just about be considered to be an outpost of Croydon.

Near to Caterham, in **GODSTONE ROAD**, there stand some mid-Victorian houses which were probably the "much sought after" properties of their day. One of these houses was bought by a Mrs Betty Sharpe in 1880 and she lived there, apparently very contentedly until she died in 1957.

Shortly after her death, the property was sold to a married couple. One day when the newcomers were busily arranging the house to their satisfaction, the husband glanced up the stairs and was amazed to see an old lady watching him from the landing. She was wearing a long Victorian dress and a lace shawl tucked neatly about her shoulders. Surprised as he was he managed to say 'Hello' to the unexpected visitor who, smiling in return, slowly disappeared. Thinking it might scare her he thought it best not to tell his wife, but shortly afterwards she also saw the old lady in exactly the same spot. They agreed that the visitations were of a friendly nature and that the spectre brought a feeling of warmth and happiness to the house.

Whilst the couple considered her a welcome visitor they refrained from mentioning her to guests, so were amazed when one day their young niece who was holidaying with them asked the name of the old lady she had met on the stairs. They told the child that they believed her to be the ghost of Betty Sharpe and need not have worried that the child would be frightened as she agreed that her presence was a friendly one.

⚛

High on the hills above the Caterham by-pass, is lonely **TILLINGDOWN FARM**. During the 1960s the local paper reported the terrifying experiences of at least two motorists whilst driving along the by-pass at night. In each incident the motorist had seen what appeared to be a man walk directly into the path of their cars. Fearing that they had killed him they got out to investigate but found nothing. Soon afterwards a gentleman in conversation with the farmer's wife mentioned the reports to her and she immediately identified the figure as being the ghost of a shepherd who had lived in one of the farm cottages and died early this century. Since then he had been a frequent visitor to the farm where he would stand at the bottom of the garden and whistle to the dog. This invariably caused the dog to become very agitated and to whine and scratch at the door in an effort to get out. One night the door was not sufficiently secured and the dog escaped, rushing to join the shepherd, who quickly led him away.

The next morning as dawn broke, the dog was found lying dead on the by-pass having been run over. After that the family never dared keep a dog.

62

CHAPTER XI — THE OLD RECTORY, CATERHAM

Though strictly belonging to the last chapter, the **'OLD RECTORY'** just has to have a chapter of its own. Now completely renovated and used as offices by a commercial firm, the 'Old Rectory' at Caterham-on-the-Hill must surely be the most haunted house in the district. Dating in part from the sixteenth century, it was once in the possession of Waltham Abbey. Though hauntings may have begun earlier, the record of mysterious circumstances start at the beginning of this century with the Reverend Alick St John Heard and his wife who moved into the rectory when his father Prebendary Heard retired to the West Country.

To begin with they could hear footsteps going along the first floor corridor when they were alone in the house. Puzzling as this was more curious events were to follow. They so often found doors open when they knew for sure that they had been closed that the Rector decided to conduct an experiment. He locked every door securely then he and his wife went out taking the keys with them. On their return about an hour later, they found every door wide open.

One day when Mrs Heard was in the bathroom situated at the end of the first floor corridor, she heard approaching footsteps and the rattle of the door knob. Believing someone to be there she called out but there was no reply. She went to open the door but was prevented from doing so as it seemed as if it was being held on the outside. She persevered and after an almighty tug the door flew inwards revealing an empty corridor. Another time as she was about to leave the bathroom the door suddenly slammed shut in her face for no apparent reason. Next to the bathroom was a bedroom with two huge bolts and a metal bar which slotted across on the inside. Obviously a previous occupant had wanted to keep someone or something out. When this bedroom was being decorated some years later the painter who came from another area and knew nothing about the ghost, found the atmosphere so depressing that he could not work in it for any length of time without having a break to restore his nerves.

The Old Rectory, Caterham:
'A bell, a monk, a little child . . .'

The rector employed a resident housekeeper with two children all of whom were repeatedly made aware of the supernatural presence. One evening the Heards were going out and they asked the housekeeper to put their supper on the table as soon as they returned. When they arrived home, they were surprised and some- what annoyed to find the meal already on the table and getting cold. They called the housekeeper to complain but she apologised and said that she was sure she had heard them walking about upstairs some time before.

On another occasion, a lady arrived at the front door saying that she had come to receive religious instruction from the Rector. The housekeeper said that as he was out, she was welcome to come in and wait until he returned. No sooner had she sat down than an elderly gentleman entered, had some brief conversation with her and left. When the Rector returned she described the visitor to him but he was completely perplexed and said he had no knowledge of such a person. When asked, the housekeeper said she had admitted nobody but the young lady.

Another extraordinary incident took place when the Reverend Heard was called away to visit his father who was desperately ill. During his absence, the verger was talking to an acquaintance in the churchyard when he was surprised to see the figure of Reverend Heard's father enter the mortuary. Having a lot on his mind at the time, the verger forgot the incident but a day or so later, he was told that the sick man had died at his home at exactly the same time as he was seen to enter the mortuary. Shortly after, the son of the housekeeper, sleeping in his own room at the rectory, awoke to find the ghost of Prebendary Heard rummaging through some papers at the end of the bed. Why had his ghost returned to the rectory? Had he left something important behind him when he retired so long ago?

Over the years both the Heards and their housekeeper became accustomed to their ghosts. Although no positive description was given of any of them, a gentleman who spent a few nights there expressed his regret to a friend, that he had slept so well that he had missed seeing the ghost which he believed to be a hooded figure resembling a monk.

When the Reverand Heard retired, he was succeeded by a Dr. Butterworth who maintained that at no time did he experience anything unusual. With the arrival of the next Rector, Reverend Kenneth Budd, the mysterious activities resumed. Although he and his wife were sceptical at first, it was not long before they had reason to change their minds.

The Rectory had been converted to flats with the Rector living on the first floor and an engineer and his family living below. One day Reverend Budd returned to the house with a friend only to find Mrs Budd had gone out taking the key with her, so they had no alternative but to wait for her return. Whilst standing on the lawn, they saw what appeared to be people moving around upstairs. They hurried over to check the doors in case they had not noticed Mrs Budd return, but they were still locked. When Mrs Budd did arrive they conducted a thorough search but found no-one on the premises.

The engineer told the architect responsible for the alterations to the building that he often heard footsteps going along the first floor corridor when the Rector was out and that they too, repeatedly found doors that they had locked wide open on their return. He said that one day when his wife was working on the hearth in front of the fireplace, she heard someone enter the room and presuming it to be her husband she turned round to see what he wanted but found she was quite alone and the door still closed.

So much supernatural activity took place that the engineer's daughter decided to call in a medium. After spending some time in the house, she said that she felt it had been used as a resting place for monks on long journeys. Something had gone wrong during one of their visits and a bell had been buried on the premises for which a monk had been searching ever since.

The Rector and his wife moved to a newly-built rectory and the engineers family left. A new occupant was found for the upper flat but the ground floor remained empty for a long time before it received new tenants. These were a family of four children and their mother. The first horrors they had to contend with were those of damp and dry rot so builders were soon called in.

Whilst the necessary repairs were being executed, the mother slept in the hall. One night she awoke with a start to find herself in a cold sweat. She was sure somebody was standing over her. Though too terrified to turn on the light, she was convinced it was a tall hooded figure. The next day she told the builder who said he was not at all surprised. He said the house had a depressing atmosphere especially at the back. Not wanting to scare the children she did not mention it to them but it wasn't long before they had stories to tell her. The son who slept at the end of the hall, said that he had heard footsteps approaching and had seen the bedroom handle move but nobody entered. He refused to sleep in the room again unless accompanied by his dog. The youngest daughter saw what she thought was a monk pass the side window and thinking it was a visitor went to let him in but he had vanished. They often thought they heard the back door open but their welcoming calls would bring no response.

Eventually the mother re-married and the husband joined the family in the rectory. This in no way deterred the resident spirits. The husband's first encounter was one evening as he was sitting alone watching television. On the sideboard was a deep glass fruit bowl, at the bottom of which were a few apples. His viewing was distracted by a dull thud and on looking towards the sideboard, he saw one of the apples rolling across the floor apparently having lifted itself out of the bowl. He did not stop to look for an explanation but rushed from the room and was glad when the family returned.

Though they continued to be disturbed by some of the happenings, particularly those that occured at the back of the house where it was constantly cold, they began to be amused by the more bizarre events. One evening as one of the teenage girls sat alone in the house with her boyfriend, they saw a pair of shoes walk as if worn by some unseen person, from one side of the room to the other. Another time the mother expected to hear howls of disgust when her son came in from work to discover that the shoes he had ordered from a mail order company were a quite hideous colour. When nothing happened she tip-toed to his room, but he wasn't there. So who had walked up the hall and into his bedroom? Frequently small articles such as hairbrushes would seem to move of their own accord and the dog would have bouts of restlessness, wandering from room to room as if following someone. The family named the friendly ghost 'Alfie' but preferred to keep anonymous the sinister 'something' that lurked in the shadows at the back of the house.

The occupants of the first floor flat were no less troubled than the family below. They too found objects would move without explanation. On returning from a holiday they found all the windows of their flat open. Pleased at first, as they had asked a friend to air the rooms, they were less pleased when he hurried up the drive behind them apologising profusely for being so late in attending to the task. Inside nothing had been taken or disturbed although the family below had heard footsteps, furniture being moved about, and on one occasion what sounded like a pile of books crashing to the floor.

Another medium visited the house and like the previous one said it had been used as a hostelry. She declared the front of the building to be possessed by the spirits of good and those at the back to be evil. She said that she felt some body or some bodies to be buried in close proximity to the house and I have information from another source which says a skeleton was recovered from a shallow grave by the back door. Perhaps it was a child's grave as a medium said she could see a figure of a child in Victorian costume following one of the daughters around the house.

Close neighbours have their own stories about the building and one concerns a young lady who lived there many years ago. She is said to have been a brilliant pianist who became desperately ill. When she died, her lover was so distraught that he committed suicide. Since then haunting music has been heard drifting across the gardens when the house was unoccupied.

I recently re-visited the old rectory. To see it now makes it difficult to believe it was haunted, but I knew it before the decorators got to work. I remember an old oak door studded with nails, one for every person who died when the Plague hit Caterham. I have seen the mists swirl round the ancient apple tree and felt the damp chill rise from the cellar. But mostly I remember the warm atmosphere at Christmas time, when a huge, traditionally decorated tree stood twinkling by the hearth, and the New Year parties that had all the right ingredients, good food, good company, and the perfect hosts.

Those days have gone and the spirits with them; or have they? For who knows what happens after the staff have left at night and before they return in the morning?

CHAPTER XII – CHALDON

Not far from Caterham-on-the-Hill, is the village of **CHALDON**. It is set in a pleasant rural area where in spite of some modern additions the past lingers on. To walk up the lane from the church on a tranquil Autumn morning, with the sun shining mistily through the trees, is quite delightful, and when dusk falls it would seem that departed spirits also find it an agreeable environment, but I was saddened by the following story told to me by a local resident.

He said that one evening, he was walking his dog near the crossroads, when he was startled to see what appeared to be six darkly clad monks drift silently across Rook Lane and enter a field where a path runs diagonally to Tollsworth Manor. He hurried towards the field in order to get a closer look but there was nothing to be seen except the grey mists of evening. Suddenly remembering his dog he glanced round to see what effect the spectres may have had on him but he was nowhere to be seen. A few minutes later there was a squeal of brakes and he saw his dog lying on the road. It was still alive but died some time later.

Had these figures been a portent of death I did wonder as I had seen a similar hooded figure sitting by my Mother's bed. Although it was only there for a fraction of a second I knew it was Death and she died two days later.

Intrigued by the Chaldon mystery, I checked the position of the sighting on an Ordnance Survey map and was excited to see that it was close to an open space called Six Brothers Field. Knowing Tollsworth Manor to have been owned once by the Abbey of Chertsey and later by

Merton Priory, I jumped to the conclusion that the six figures the gentleman had seen were the "Brothers" going back to their home after toiling in the fields. My assumption was however incorrect. On looking through a local history book I discovered the field to have much more recent history. It had been presented to the National Trust by a local builder in memory of himself and his five brothers, one of whom had won the V.C. in the Second World War. So much for an interesting theory!

⚠

It is good to know that ghosts are not necessarily unhappy or out for revenge. The ghostly gatherings at **THE ROOKERY** in Chaldon, appear to have been of an exceedingly jocular nature. I was told that some years ago, this house was occupied by a widow and several of her children. Being in a rural area, the house was surrounded by trees and much vegetation so it is unlikely that sounds would carry from other buildings in the vicinity. Nevertheless, it would seem that on various occasions, the family, having retired to bed, were disturbed by what sounded like a noisy dinner party in the rooms below. There would be loud laughter, music and singing and the clatter of crockery. Any one of the family with the courage to creep down the stairs to investigate, only discovered silent, empty rooms.

The cause of these disturbances were never discovered but my correspondent who lived in the locality, said they did not pay too much attention to the reports as the ladies of the family were "somewhat inclined to tell psychic stories".

⚠

Now used as a nursing home where, I am assured, there is a warm friendly atmosphere, the **'GLEBE HOUSE'** in Church Lane was once the setting for some very strange events. Though there are still fragments of an earlier building the major portion was constructed in the late eighteenth century with big extensions in the twentieth century. It had been the Chaldon rectory, but when my informant's father purchased the house from the Church in 1927 he was asked to change the name for fear of postal complications.

When the family went to view the house, they noticed that none of the bedrooms in the Eighteenth century section had been occupied. Thinking this was rather curious, the mother asked the Rector's wife if there were any ghosts about. She looked acutely embarrassed and mumbling an inaudible reply she hurried out of the room.

The family settled in and a son and daughter had no qualms about being allocated two of the previously unused bedrooms. These rooms were adjacent, divided only by a thin wall through which sound carried easily. Everything seemed fine until one Summer morning when the son went down to breakfast. His mother looked at him inquiringly and asked why he had gone into the garden in the night playing his piccolo. The son replied that he had done no such thing and that as of that time he hadn't even learned to play it. His mother was unbelieving but decided it was best not to pursue the matter.

Some time later, the son woke one morning unusally early. Glancing at his clock he saw it was 6 a.m. and decided it was far too early to get up. For a while he lay there wondering what had disturbed him, but finding no explanation he turned over and went to sleep again. At breakfast it was his sister's turn to look curious. She asked him what he had done to cause the noise that sounded like the clanging of bells in the early hours of the morning. He replied that although he had woken early he had done and heard nothing. She wasn't convinced as she said she had heard him moving about at the time.

The years passed peacefully and it seemed that whatever spirits had been disturbed by their arrival had now gone to rest. The son married in 1935 and moved to another district, only seeing the family when he called in from time to time. One evening he arrived rather late, to find his mother and two sisters in a great state of agitation. The sister who had previously heard the clanging bells had continued to sleep in the same bedroom without further disturbance until early that morning. She had woken with a start to find a man standing over her. At first she thought it was her father waiting to rebuke her for something that she had forgotten. He said nothing so she raised herself slightly from the bed in order to get a closer view. It was then that she realised it was not her father but a man dressed in a black gown with white braids as worn by the clergy in the Eighteenth century. A greenish light rose from the ground enveloping the lower part of the figure and as she stared wide-eyed he glided slowly and silently out of the room.

After this unnerving episode, she was very reluctant to return to her room, but on further consideration she realised she had come to no harm so decided she would and nothing ever happened again. Obviously the Rector's wife had known something but whatever it was she hadn't been prepared to tell.

CHAPTER XIII – WARLINGHAM

The village of Warlingham is within easy reach of Croydon. It still has its village green and a charming old public house called "The White Lion".

Beyond the village at the junction of Limpsfield Road and Slines Oak Road is a small pond now very overgrown with weeds. This was once the scene of a disastrous coaching accident. It happened almost a century ago as the coach carrying four passengers headed towards Croydon. A highwayman lurking behind the bushes is said to have dashed forward frightening the horses so much that they bolted into the pond dragging the coach behind them. All four passengers and the coachman were drowned. Although nothing has been seen lately, there used to be reports from people who had seen the coach rise from the murky depths of the pond, its lights blazing and the passengers screaming. Certainly something to think about if you are passing Slines Green pond in the early evening as darkness creeps on and the damp mist swirls among the reeds.

My last story also comes from the Warlingham area. It is a tale for telling at Christmas time, preferably when the listeners are seated together round a glowing fire. A lady who moved into her house in **FARLEIGH ROAD** about twenty years ago told me that she soon noticed that local residents always referred to one section of the road as **BAKER'S HILL**. When she asked an elderly neighbour the reason for this she was very surprised at the following explanation.

Apparently there was a bakery in the vicinity from which the baker's boy regularly walked to Selsdon to deliver to the customers. One day as he passed some trees on the bend of the road he was set upon by a woodman wielding an axe who then hacked him to death.

Apart from a nervous glance towards the trees on Baker's Hill whenever she was passing, the lady gave no more thought to the story. But some years later her daughter, who was resident in Selsdon, said that some neighbours had experienced a very frightening encounter. It happened on Boxing Day when the neighbour drove his father and son to Westerham. A thick grey fog clung to the trees and brushed against the car as they motored up Farleigh Road. Suddenly a dark shape loomed up in front of them and the headlights revealed the figure of a tall man wearing a country style suit and carrying an axe in his right hand. The driver slammed on his brakes and jumped out of the car to shout at the man for being in the road and endangering all their lives, but he had vanished. Nothing was to be seen but the trees dripping with moisture as they hung over the open road. All three passengers had seen the apparition and were so shaken that they used an alternative route on the return journey in order to avoid a second encounter.

When the lady told another elderly resident about the family's ordeal, she said that her mother had been seventeen years old at the time of the murder and had told her the exact tree where the axe had been hidden. Since then, whenever she had passed that spot with her dog, he had panicked and run as if his life was threatened.

Fortunately for today's motorists, the trees have now been removed and the road widened, making driving easier and ghosts less likely.

CHAPTER XIV — ENTER THE COLONEL

And how does my own personal story continue? Well, as I have already stated, I crept forward and upward, one stair at a time. Though very apprehensive I was convinced I would find a logical explanation for our nightly disturbances, pigeons perhaps, or maybe a squirrel. I avoided the thought of rats. As I reached the top of the stairs, I switched on the torch. Its powerful beam pierced the darkeness and illuminated every corner but there was nothing. I waited for a while in case the noises should start again. Yes, I felt intensely cold and my hair was beginning to stand on end, but still nothing happened.

Returning to the children who were waiting anxiously below, I had to admit defeat. As we sat wondering what to do next, one of my daughters suddenly asked what I had done with the things I had found in the attic when we first moved in. For the moment I could not think what she was referring to, then I remembered the silver topped army baton I had found in a dark corner and the hip flask with its rotting leather case that the plumber had found at the bottom of the old water tank when he was in the process of removing it. I replied that I had brought them down and left them in a cupboard where they were waiting to be cleaned. She suggested I clean them quickly and replace them in the attic in case the noises were caused by a ghost searching for his personal property.

This idea sparked off the family's imagination, we soon built up a picture of a colonel who had once lived in the house and had acquired the habit of slipping up to the attic for a quick drink from his hip flask whenever he got the opportunity. We imagined that on one occasion he may have been surprised by his wife so that he had hastily slipped the flask into the tank where it had remained for many years.

The next morning I scrubbed and polished the articles until they shone like new then returned them to the attic. I hung the baton on the wall suspended by a red silk cord and placed the hip flask on a shelf beside it. That evening we waited to see if the noises would start as usual, but they didn't, nor have we heard them since.

Eventually the attic was attractively decorated and transformed into a bedroom for guests. My first visitor was an actress playing at the Ashcroft Theatre. She was delighted with the room and when she came down the next morning, I asked her how well she had slept. At first she said very well, then she said that although she had fallen asleep quickly, she had been woken by a slow tapping sound and had felt she was not alone. She had put on the light but seen nothing so had gone to sleep again. I laughed and suggested it may have been the "colonel" whereupon she asked to be told the story.

She stayed for two weeks and said she was often aware of some presence but was never scared as she was convinced he was a friendly, if somewhat eccentric old gentleman. When she moved on to her new digs she wrote that although she was quite comfortable she greatly missed the "old colonel". Since then many peole have slept there, some have commented on the atmosphere, others have not. One of my children who spent a night in the attic said she would never do so again, especially as she was sure something had touched her on the shoulder. I now use the room as my studio where I work and sleep. I hear no unusual sounds but have sometimes felt a gentle touch on my shoulder and have spun round expecting to find somebody standing behind me only to find the room quite empty.

Do I believe in ghosts? I still do not know, but would I remove the baton and hip flask? I think not. Do you believe in ghosts? Maybe you are as convinced of their existence as was a lady that I spoke to in Caterham or perhaps you agree with the old gardener I met in Kenley who on being asked what he knew about ghosts replied vehemently, "Ghosts?" I don't know nothing about ghosts, they're just a load of old bunk!"

⚛

ACKNOWLEDGEMENTS

Roger Packham, 'The Bourne Society'

Paul Sowan, 'Croydon Natural History and Scientific Society'

M. Marshall, 'The Croydon Airport Society'

Joan Warwick, 'The Norwood Society'

M. Alexander, Guildford Museum.

E. Pratt and Staff of the East Surrey Museum.

The Sisters and Staff of Virgo Fidelis Convent school.

The Staff and Headmaster of St Joseph's College.

The Croydon Advertiser.

The News and Property News.

The Archives Department, Brixton.

The Librarians of Croydon, Caterham, Brixton, Norbury, Thornton Heath, Upper Norwood and Wallington libraries

Croydon Parish Church.

Friends of the Old Palace.

Jim Lawless of 'Goody's Wine Bar', Staff at the 'Royal Oak' and the 'Wheatsheaf Inn'

Mrs Gilliam, Maisie Dance, Daphne Moss, Nora Calvert, Beki Stewart, Mrs Stoff, Ken Saunders, Sarah-Jane Stewart, Graham Mason, Mrs Walker, Mrs E.C. Williams, Roger Gamell, Robert Ball, Mr Guy Hereward, Mrs Budd-Pickard, Mr George Baker, Mrs Garrish, Mr Peter Randell, Georgina and Terry Martin and family, Dagmar Glausnitzer, Mr Amos, Mr Tidy, Mr Hall, Miss Squier, Mr Fuller, Mrs P. Fretwell, Mrs C. Russell, Margaret Merrington, Mr John Adams, Mrs Barbara Owen, Mr John Booth, Mr R. Riddett.

And a special thank you to the lady in Kenley who knew nothing about the local ghosts but recognised a thirsty person when she saw one and kindly invited me in for refreshment on one of the only warm days in the Summer of 1988.

BIBLIOGRAPHY

BARDENS Dennis, "Ghosts and Hauntings"

BENTHAM T., "A History of Beddington"

CLUETT D., NASH J., LEARMOUTH R., "Croydon Airport — 1928-1939, The Great Days"

FODOR Nandor (DR), "On the Trail of the Poltergeist"

GREEN Andrew, "Our Haunted Kindgom" 1974

GREEN Andrew, "Ghosts of the South East" 1976

GREEN Andrew, "Phantom Ladies" 1977

HALLAM Jack, "Ghosts of London"

HERBERT W.B., "Railway Ghosts". 1985

INDEX

INDEX